CREDIT SECRETS:
CREDIT REPAIR REVELED
M. BLEVINS
Copyright 2014 by M. BLEVINS

Congratulations! You have decided to take a step toward repairing your credit. For whatever the reason you have decided to do this, you need to pat yourself on the back. You have learned that your credit is an important extension of yourself. Your credit, in this day and age, is your "identity" when it comes to banking and loan institutions. Seldom will you find, anymore, the bank that will provide you credit based on your relationship with them and reputation. There is nothing more frustrating than needing a new car and unable to buy one without good credit unless you have enough money to "buy" credit. This is why "Buy Here Pay Here" car lots are as abundant, as these businesses are aware that around 70% of Americans have damaged credit. With the recent years of recession the average credit score among Americans have dropped. These businesses are laughing all the way to the bank with their high interest rates, high car prices and large down payments requirements. Many of these companies are pushing the Federal Usury Laws if not outright violating them. With a poor credit score your negotiating powers with these companies is all but gone and you can get stuck with a subpar car that they are willing to repossess at the slightest hint of financial trouble. As unethical as this practice is, it is legal.

In taking the initiative in controlling your credit, you are empowering yourself to save money, and a lot of it, over the next few years and potentially a lifetime. This process is not an overnight process, however, is just a few short hours you can learn what you need to better protect yourself from deceptive collection practices and in no time. Usually in around 6-9 months you can have a credit score worthy of a home loan (Fico score of 640+)

Why is it important to know my rights regarding credit collections?

Here is a money saving tip that you will want to practice from here on out. Collection companies violate Fair Credit Reporting Act, Fair Debt Collection Act and Usury Laws with their practices. Debt collectors buys bulk accounts for pennies on the dollar and any money they obtain from their collection practices is mainly profit. These are known as zombie debts, because the debt has been unable to be paid back by the consumer, and many are past statute of limitation on collecting (this will be discussed later). They have been known to curse, threaten, lie, and harass consumers. They will tell you the only way to get items off your credit are to pay them, which is untrue. Negative credit accounts with the exceptions of Judgments, Liens, Bankruptcy and Student Loans, will be removed seven (7) years from the last PAYMENT date. In order to protect their investment, creditors will not disclose this information and will blatantly lie if asked the ways accounts can be removed. Let's give an example here.

If you owe Bank A $2500 from a credit card that you were unable to pay. Your last payment of $25 was made in October 2010. With the seven year law, this account would be scheduled to drop off your credit in October of 2017. They have decided they cannot collect and sale the account to a debt collector.

So, Bank A sells the "zombie debt" to Collector B. Collector B changes the account number of the account, the date of last activity (in this case October 2010) to the date they acquired the debt, say January of 2014, and then they unilaterally decide that your $2500 debt to Bank A is now worth $7000 (this is a real scenario I have seen). You see this account on your credit and are not sure what this is, so you call the debt collector. By this time, they have already sent you notices of this debt by mail and have probably gave you 30 days to dispute the item, otherwise you agree to the debt by "admission by silence." Basically, they are saying that since you didn't dispute this, you agree that this item is your debt and therefore, your responsibility. You probably threw the notice out as many people do with mail they don't know or if they are aware it's an old debt that they can't pay. They may even begin calling you several times a day until you pick up the phone. Technically speaking, the laws that are designed to protect the consumer are being violated in every aspect of this scenario.

When you speak to a representative from the company they are generally very forceful in their language. They will first ask you to verify your personal information. They do this for a few different reasons. If you verify your information, they have an affirmative defense that the account is yours. Also, if they cannot verify your personal information, then they are violating another law that protects your privacy if they continue the conversation. They also have to identify that they are "a debt collector attempting to collect a debt and all information collected is in an effort to collect the debt." If they do not inform you of this, it's another violation of the law. So, already in this scenario several violations could have been made.

After the preliminary introduction, you finally get down to business. The collector is going to connive, convince, and potentially coerce you to make a payment on your account. They attack your character for not paying the account if you give resistance and may violate the laws with threats of jail time or taking personal property. If you pay any money be it, $1 or $1000, you have just re-aged your account. Instead of the account falling off in October of 2017, you have re-aged the account to seven (7) years from the date of the payment, say February 2014. So now your drop off date is February 2021. This also re-ages this account on your credit which instead shows that instead of four years ago, only 4 months ago you were delinquent on your account, therefore, dropping your credit score. So why would a person do this to themselves? The simple answer is that people don't understand the system. This is why utilizing credit repair is better off than paying the debt.

When you are dealing with statute of limitations, there are a few dates to consider. The first is the date the original item is due to drop off your credit. We have already discussed the seven (7) year rule. The next date is the statue of limitations on filing a judgment in the court. In the state of Texas, the statute of limitation on suing for a debt is four (4) years from the date of the original delinquency. This means, that in our scenario that after October of 2014 if you live in Texas, you cannot be sued for this particular debt. Now, if the creditor re-ages the debt legally or illegally, they can sue you in court and if you do not respond or challenge the dispute, then they obtain a default judgment and you are then legally liable for the debt. You can fight an illegally obtained judgment, but by this time, the cost may be more than the actual debt. In many cases, if you don't own property such as a house, land, etc., many creditors won't bother with the cost of the judgment because there is nothing to hold you to the debt. If you are a home or land owner, you will not be able to sale your property until the debt is paid, out of closing cost or otherwise. That's not to say that they won't file a judgment against you. Once a judgment is filed, it may drop off your credit report but it will be in court records and in some cases, indefinitely. Some states allow wage garnishments, so if you have an judgment against you, they can file with the court to take up to a certain percentage of your "disposal" income. Disposable income is your income after they take out taxes and insurance, so basically your net income. In some cases, it can be 25% or more until the debt is paid. You should check the statue of limitations of your state and whether or not they allow wage garnishment. This should be taken into consideration when repairing your credit.

In many cases, once you start credit repair, previously old debts that haven't had any activity in a few years may, all of a sudden, become active by selling the debt to a debt collector. This is in response to a challenge to the debt. This happened to a client of mine with an old credit card. One month after a dispute on her credit report, her account was now with a new collector and over $4000 was added to the account. The account has only nine more months under the statute of limitations for dropping off but the collector attempted to re-age the debt illegally. By law, all information on a credit report must be correct.

In this case, the statue of limitations to sue for the debt is long past, and therefore, there is no incentive to make a payment on this account. Threats to sue by the company at this point would be a violation of the Fair Debt Collection Act. Her options at this time are to wait for the nine months to expire or to go ahead and dispute the account with the credit bureaus. In this case, the creditor stated that the account was correct and no changes were made. When this happens, you must dispute with the creditor company with a request for validation. During a validation, they must in writing "prove" this debt is yours. Failure to do so requires them to have it removed from the credit report. In some cases, they will not "prove" the account, but rather just state that the account was verified which does not meet the legal requirements for them to continue reporting the bad debt. At this point, they are in violation and can be sued for violation of the Fair Credit Reporting Act.

Credit Bureaus: Why do they not delete items that are wrong?

The credit bureaus, Experian, Equifax, and TransUnion are cash cows. They have made billions of dollars on their disputing practices. If you have ever disputed an incorrect item on your credit file with one of these companies and they have not removed the item, it's for good reason, at least for the bureaus.

You cannot have an item reportedly correctly removed from your credit legally with the exception of the expiration of the debt. However, in many of the credit reports, 70% or more of the items have inaccurate dates, changed account numbers, no name reported, or other information that is inaccurate, which is all grounds for a dispute with the credit bureaus.

Credit bureaus are regulated by the Federal Trade Commission (FTC) and can be sued for violation the federal laws protecting the consumers. There are hundreds of lawsuits filed everyday against bureaus for failure to report accurate information. This is multi-million/billion dollar industry. They charge creditors for placing accounts in their files. Also, they charge the creditor for each dispute that is made. They have little incentive to remove items. The way the bureaus work exactly is not widely known as it is proprietary information; however, much of the process is automated, from the arrival of the letter to the final dispute decision. Letters are scanned, placed in a computer and awaits a response from the creditor. The bureaus do not investigate or validate disputes as required by law, hence all the lawsuits, but whether due to consumer ignorance or misinformation, the average consumer is not aware of the violations and this makes it very profitable for the credit bureaus to continue their practices. Best practice is to get your dispute into the hands of a human at the bureaus not just scanned through a computer. This will give you a better chance of the dispute being removed either due to time limitation or someone adding a personal approach to the dispute.

Statically, the average consumer will stop disputing items on their credit report after 90 days. The creditors bank on this and will stall. The process can be frustrating, but in the end worth it. In this book, you will be provided letters to the credit bureaus, letters to the creditors, and tips on how to use them.

Be patient, follow through, and Good LUCK!

TIPS: Best ways to dispute with creditors and credit bureaus

Online Disputes-Do not dispute online. Do not agree with any bureau to complete disputes online. In doing so, you surrender certain rights for disputing. They don't tell you this when they send an email requesting to allow all further disputes to be online.

You want to always hand-write your envelopes. You specifically do not want to use preprinted address labels. Though this takes less time than handwriting, it will not help you get your letter into the hands of a real person which is the goal. If this doesn't happen, your dispute will be filed and scanned with the thousands of other letters that is sent every day. You really want to stand out.

Along with your dispute letter you want to send a copy of a recent (within 30 days) utility bill in your name with a copy of your driver's license or picture identification and a copy of your social security card. This lets the bureaus know that you are who you say you are and in many cases bureaus won't open a case without this information.

On each and every letter you will want to change up the font, text color, formatting on each dispute. This is especially true if you are disputing more than your own credit report say a spouse, friend or family member. This again, will help get past that pesky scanner.

You will also want to change up each wording on the letters to the different bureaus. Again, those pesky scanners are the reason why. The scanners scan for key phrases that are being repeated to try to weed out credit repair companies or novices who are using form letters in order to try to prevent the dispute from being considered. Though it is your right to use a credit repair company, the bureaus will try to stall. They do not want consumer to have an "edge" with experts helping you. This reduces their effectiveness to stall and increased law suites when they violate the law. Each letter needs to be personalized to get into someone's hand in order to have a better chance of having your negative items deleted.

Do not want dispute more than five items at any given time-Each dispute takes around 45 days. The credit bureaus and creditors have 30 days from date of receipt of letter to investigate and provide results of a dispute.

Disputing more than five (5) items at a time (per bureau) can land you in the "fraudulent dispute" pile and your dispute will not be investigated. There is law that allows the bureaus off the hook if they can prove your dispute is fraudulent. The general advice that non-credit experts tell you to do when you dispute items on your report, is to "dispute everything" and say "it's not yours." This is technically illegal on your behalf if you do this. That is why the bureaus are ready to utilize the law on their side. They can even prevent you from filing a legitimate dispute for some time. If you have utilized this tactic in the past, and it worked, they are not likely to allow this to happen again. If it didn't work, then you have likely been "flagged" as a frivolous disputer. At this point, you would need to seek the help of someone who is more skilled in filing disputes, such as a lawyer or credit specialist, in order to fix the issue. You can do it yourself, but as a DIY'er, you're not likely to know the trade secrets to get past this. In reality, many credit repair companies that offer "guarantees" won't even take you on as a client unless it's been a year or more since you "tried" to fix your credit yourself. You don't want to cut off your nose to spite your face here. You need to be an educated disputer.

You are always going to want to dispute with the credit bureaus first. This can obtain the most results in the shortest amount of time. Also, you have ammunition against the creditors for the next step of disputing.

You are also always going to send your letters Certified Mail. Return receipt is not required but suggested. This is the only way to "prove" that you have actually communicated with the different agencies. Depending on how many letters you send, this process can get expensive. Sending Certified Mail ensures the letter is able to be tracked and reduces the cost of disputing. You will want to have Return Receipt service if you are certain the creditor violated any laws and are refusing to remove the disputed item.

If you find an item that you are certain is not yours, you have an address that is not yours on your report, or a different social security number or date of birth, you might be a victim of identity theft. This is one of the number one growing crimes that is out there to date. It's easy to do for any savvy criminal and difficult to fight, once it happens to you. There are horror stories of people who have lost everything due to fighting identity theft. Elderly people are the most at risk. I have encounter a person during my time in sales attempting to buy a car who had been flagged as having a flagged social security card. But this was only after he had bought three cars. He was in this country illegally and was using an 80 year old ladies social security card. She never even had a clue. I have a few more stories like that. Sadly they are too numerous.

If you do find that you may be a victim of identity theft, you will want to first, ile a police report. You will need to get a copy of the report and send an enlarged color photo of your driver's license or picture identification and social security charge with the police report to each credit bureau. During this process, take the time to dispute all negative items (this is the only time you should dispute more than five items). You don't want to lie and say everything is not your, but you can use phrasing such as, "I'm not sure what this item is." This leaves the ball in the bureaus court to prove it is yours. You may catch a break here.

With identity theft being such a hot topic, the bureaus will take you seriously with a police report. Since identity theft is so prominent, it is hard to catch and prosecute the criminal. So even if you know who stole your identity, be it a friend or family members (yes this happens), then you shouldn't feel bad about filing the report. You shouldn't allow yourself to be victimized for any reason.

If you have started a round of disputes, you will want to wait for each round to be completed before starting next round. You don't want to delay the process by sending multiple requests. This will show that you are "too" eager to try to beat out the credit bureaus.

By law, the bureaus are not allowed to merge spouse's credit reports without a written request; however, this happens all the time. If this has happened to you, you will specifically tell the bureaus that you did not authorize a merge report and demand they remove the spouses' items, especially if the account is a negative account. This is a different scenario than being a co-signer or an authorized user on an account. If you are a co-signer or an authorized using on a credit account, even if the primary person responsible defaults or becomes delinquent, it will be documented on your report. Be careful who you allow on your accounts and who you allow to put your on their report.

Did you know that there was such a thing as ChexSystems? You probably did if you have tried to recently use a check at a retailer. It's the system that the machine runs your check through in order to approve or decline a check. It is also used by backs to determine if you are a good "banking" client.

You are allowed to review your ChexSystems report, just like accredit report. ChexSystems could be preventing you from cashing a check, getting a bank account or obtaining a loan. You have the same rights with ChexSystems as you do with the credit bureaus and the process is the same. This is discussed later in this book.

If you have medical accounts on your credit, HIPPA letters can be very powerful. Many believe that medical bills are not allowed to be on your credit report; however, this is just false. It is a debt that you owe; however, as a consumer you are protected by the HIPPA Act, which mandates privacy for the consumer regarding medical treatment, from having certain information disclosed. Third party debt collectors are not allowed any information that has a diagnosis disclosed, but you do not know what they have, until you ask. In many cases, if you ask for documentation of their records on you, they will stop reporting the account to the credit bureau and stall because they are required to provide ALL information on you and it is a violation of the law if they don't disclose what they have. Chances are they were given invoices, if they were given anything, with your diagnosis or treatment code documented on the forms. Without explicit consent by you for a third party to have your medical information, any information that they hold that has this, is a violation of the law and your rights. They don't want to be in violation of the law, so to keep from you digging further; they will delete these items off your report.

When you are trying to repair your credit, you do not want to do anything that will stop or jeapordize the process. People sabotage their efforts when they decide to take their dispute over the phone. You do not want to discuss an account over the phone.

Unless you are confident in what you are doing. It is better to negotiate settlements by mail. You may end up saying something that will tie you to the debt. It is best to instruct companies that all further conversations with you are to be via mail and not phone.

If a creditor is calling, get their name and address and send via certified mail a cease and desist letter from calling you. It doesn't have to be anything fancy, just require them to send all communications via mail. If after they receive this notification, calls continue, they are in violation. Simply telling them to not call does not meet the legal requirements for them to stop.

One of the quickest ways to have a negative item removed is to "Pay for Delete." You may find a time that paying for the item to be deleted will be the quickest way to repair your credit. If you have more money than time, this is not a bad option, but if you only have one or two items that you need off due to being put on hold for a loan "until it's taken care of," this can be very successful. Keep in mind all offers should be in writing without acknowledging responsibility. If the creditor tells you that it's illegal to delete the item, they are lying. The credit bureaus are required to do whatever the creditors request of them. In many cases, the creditors have an agreement with the bureaus not to delete items prematurely; however, when it comes to getting money or not, they will generally take the money. You don't want to be afraid to walk away from the offer. This can be done by phone for a faster response, but don't say "I have a debt with you." Instead use, "you claim I owe a debt." DO NOT EVER acknowledge the debt is yours.

TIPS: Best ways to Build Credit

Many people end up wrecking their credit in an attempt to get out of debt. First and foremost, never close old accounts. A key factor in credit scoring is history of open accounts, and the longer the better. If you have a credit card collecting dust, DO NOT close the account. It will only cut your credit history. You want to keep good accounts active even if you don't use them. Place a small amount $20-$30 every few months just to keep it open. This shouldn't hurt you and if it did, you have more things to worry about then repairing your credit at this time.

Debt to credit ratio, is a large portion of your credit report. There is a sweet spot when it comes to how much credit you are using vs. how much you have. Any credit card 90% utilized is considered "maxed out" and will have a negative impact on you score. A credit card with no balance has the same impact on having a card around 50% utilized. Experts suggest keeping cards lower than 30% on all accounts; however, 1% to 20% is the sweet spot.

An easy way to determine how much of your credit card is safe to use is to take you credit limit divide by 3. For example: $900/3= $300. So never spend more than $300 on this account. If you keep this in mind, you will help your score.

You are also going to want to pay down all credit card balances to less than 30%. This may take some time, but you will not improve your score overall if you keep overspending on your cards.

You have to have credit to build credit. I tell people this all the time. When they tell me they do not want any credit cards, I tell them that they are not serious about improving their credit score. This is obviously not the case if you have open credit cards already. This more for the "cash" buyers and the ones who don't "trust" themselves with credit cards. If you don't have at least three (3) open, active, good accounts, GET THEM.

If you have such a poor score that you can't get credit try a few different things. First, open a secured credit card. Yes this cost you money, but it will give you a boost. Second, have someone put you on a GOOD revolving credit account as an authorized user. As an authorized user, you will have the credit item placed on your credit report and technically, you can use the account, but you are not responsible for the payment. This is how parents have helped their children obtain credit for decades. It's legal to do this and they don't ask the relationship of the person being placed on the account. So this is helpful as long as the primary person on the account is responsible with their credit. Credit bureaus and lenders don't like "authorized users" because it manipulates the scoring system to provide an advantage to the consumer who may not otherwise have good credit, but due to consumer demand and protest, this practice is not likely to go away anytime soon.

The third way to start building credit is to open a secured line of credit. $500-$1000. Some banks offer this. The way it works is that you put up some money, the bank makes you sign a loan agreement and gives it back to you. They charge a small bit of interest, and you pay it back in small increments over 6-12 months (never do less than 6 months). At the end of this transaction, you have built credit and you have your money back minus a small cost.

One of the WORST things you can do to your credit is to get those really easy to get, really expensive to pay for payday loans. Do NOT use Payday loans/Title loans! These payday loans are terrible.

These loan terms are usually less than 6 months and wreak havoc on your credit report not to mention, being around 500% interest or more. Each time these are renewed it looks like a new account. I had a client who was able to buy a house and rebuild his credit only after he was able to pay off all his payday loans. He never realized how expensive these really were on his budget not to mention how much it hurt his credit score. He was lucky enough to have a good rapport with his local credit union that allowed him to borrow the money to help pay off his debts. This also helped him build credit with his credit union.

To bankers, payday loans looks like you are desperate for money and/or you can't afford to pay your bills. NEVER, ever, never, ever, did I say never, use this kind of loan. If you find yourself taking these out or relying on these loans to pay bills, you need to find a way to make more income. Take up a second job, walk dogs, clean houses, whatever you need to do. Put any extra money on these loans to pay them off. Once they are paid off, you can take the cost out of your budget and get back on track.

The best thing you can do for your credit is to start paying your bills on time. One late pay during your credit repair process will sabotage your efforts. Many paid credit repair company will stop working on your credit if you add anything negative to your credit or you are late on any accounts. One late pay in 24 months will kill your credit score. If the late pay has been in the past 90 days, your score has likely plummeted even if everything else is fine. One recent late pay can cost you over 100 point drop in your credit score.

My next piece of advice is not meant to discredit or look poorly on anyone or their profession, but it needs to be said. Don't assume your accountant, tax advisor, or attorney knows more about your credit than you. There is a time and place for professionals, but don't discount their motives. A bankruptcy attorney will always tell you that bankruptcy is your best option if you are underwater, but that may not be the case. You can help yourself out of that situation if you know and understand your consumer rights. In many cases, had a consumer consulted a credit restoration company, they could have avoided Bankruptcy

A Bankruptcy can stay on your credit report for up to 10 years and it hunts you the entire time. You can obtain credit after a bankruptcy, but as long as it's on your credit, the rates are not that favorable.

Accountant or tax attorneys are excellent advisors on their particular topic. Their job is to help you manage your money and taxes; however, understand this, they may NOT be educated in how certain decisions affect your credit score. For example; I had a client who is rather wealthy. She had several credit cards and loans. Her accountant, in an effort to "help," gave her advice and suggested she pay off all her credit cards, and that she close the accounts. She did what any prudent person would do and listen to the advice of the so called "expert." In doing so, she cut her credit history and debt to credit ratio. She quickly experienced over 100 point drop on her credit report. She could not at that point get approved for a home loan even though she had plenty of money. She didn't want to spend the $160,000 to buy the home outright (plus closing cost). Even wealthy people understand the importance of using credit to leverage large amount of debt. They rely on it. Even Warren Buffet "borrows" money to buy items. He stated once that, "It would be too expensive not to."

Another example of listening to the experts is this: A client was going through a very expensive divorce. Everyone knows that divorce will kill credit, but not everyone knows why. I figured it out with this client. Her attorney gave her the very specific advice to NOT pay on any of her credit cards, loans, etc, until the divorce was final because if she paid them she assumed the debt. Over $14,000 later, the couple reconciled and now both have terrible credit because of the 30+, 60+, and 90+ late pays on their credit report. She is now having a difficult time buying a house. She is working on her credit.

I spoke to several bankers who state that they hear these horror stories all the time of bad advice from "so called" professionals. The bottom line is, if you don't pay on your debt, you will ruin your credit, no matter the reason. Creditors don't care why you are not paying, just that you are not paying. Why lose your house or car if you plan on keeping it even if you are going through a divorce? This doesn't make sense to me, at least, not when it comes to protecting your credit.

The Get out of Debt plan is a great idea, but as some cost. There is a popular book, plan, program that takes you step-by-step to getting out of debt. It's a great program and I recommend it to anyone who is so far underwater with their debt, they need to make real financial changes. However, this system wrecks your credit.

I recently received a phone call from a lady who was proud to say that she has been debt free for seven (7) years. Her car, student loans, and other personal property were paid for in full, but she didn't own her home. She had paid for everything in cash and now wanted to purchase a house. To her dismay, she ended up with a credit score of a whooping "0". Zero! How does this happen? When all your debt expire and you have no credit and no debt, you end up with a zero credit score. This also happens when you are 18 years old and have never had a bill in your name or credit card. She will have to start from scratch to rebuild her credit, which will take 12-24 months at least to be able to potentially buy a home. Some people say having bad credit is better than no credit. I guess it depends on the situation.

The opposite end of this spectrum is if you have gotten out of debt recently and now that you are back on your feet, you want to buy a home or car. Since this debt plan advocates allowing your credit to take a nose dive, you will need a credit repair plan which will need to be tailor made based on the length of time it's taken you to get on your feet, amount of debt and the type of debt that has been neglected. This is why knowing your statute of limitations and the consumer protection laws are very important. Take your time to plan your strategies so you don't end up in court or you re-age debt. But there is still hope. Don't fret. You can do it.

One overlooked item that will harm your credit is Credit Inquires. There are two different types. They are soft inquires and hard inquiries. Soft inquires will not affect your credit score. This is pulled by companies for things such as pre-approval offers. This is also when you pull the credit from a credit reporting site yourself. These do not hurt your credit. Hard inquires are something different.

A hard inquire would occur when you apply for a loan or line of credit such as credit card, home loan, car loan, etc. Each hard credit inquiry is worth 3-6 points on your credit. Any time you apply for a loan, the company will insist on pulling your credit report. Each pull will go on your credit and stay on there for 24-months. Companies will say that several inquiry's in a short amount of time such as 14 days only count as one pull by a lender. Though this may be true from a lender perspective, it still affects your credit score, which overall, affects the ability to obtain a loan.

I have seen car dealerships pull your report with 10 different creditors trying to find a company to loan you the money. They turn you down at that dealership and then you go to the next one, and they pull your credit with different lenders. By this time, the first dealership has ruined your chances of obtaining a loan anywhere else. Generally speaking, if the dealership can't approve a loan with four or less inquires, they can't get the loan approval. Chances are the next dealership won't be able to either.

Don't allow this behavior. If you are in the market for a car, set specific limits on many inquires a dealership can make. This will force them to be more selective. It's your credit; you can control what is done with your credit. The best idea is to see your local bank and try to obtain a pre-approved loan and allow them to set the price amount they will authorize. The same can be said about home loan companies.

If you are trying to get a loan and you are not sure of the credit score, do yourself a favor and go to a website that allows you to pull your FICO scores (which cost money) and determine if you are eligible for a loan before you start shopping around. Remember 620 or better and you are in fair shape. A 640 or better will get you a loan. A 720 or better will get you a good rate loan. Don't drop your credit score any more by allowing companies to pull multiple reports from multiple companies. Four inquires a year is considered excessive by credit scoring terms.

The score on your credit that you need to be the most concerned with is your mid-score. Since there are three major credit bureaus, there are obviously three credit reports. A Tri-bureau report is the best way to really see where you are with your credit. When obtaining a home loan specifically, the lender will look at your mid-score, which simple is the middle of all three scores. It doesn't matter which bureau has the mid score, just what the score is. For example, if TransUnion's FICO score is a 719, Experian's FICO is a 647 and Equifax's FICO is a 639, the Experian FICO score of 647 will be used to approve the loan. It is not unusual to have a wide range of scores as each company that reports to credit bureaus will decide which if any or all credit bureaus it will report to for debt. Companies may only report to one bureau and not the others or any other combination. So for a good indicator of where you are at, you must have a tri-bureau credit report or at least a tri-bureau score.

Consumers with poor credit flock to lease-to-own companies when they need furniture, tv's, appliances, etc. There are many lease-to-own furniture companies. These companies offer to report to credit. What they don't tell you, is in many cases, they only report under two conditions: One, you completely pay off your debt and then it can take up to six months or more to report this "good" account to the credit bureaus, if they don't forget or two, you fail to pay on your debt and they are unable to retrieve the property at which point, you have a negative account on your credit report.

Many companies, who offer lease to own, may not report to credit bureaus unless you fail to pay. This may not be a good way to build credit. But it is a good way to possibly over extend your budget, so always take this into consideration if you are trying to build credit.

Many people want to know, "How do I get a Perfect credit score?"A perfect credit score is considered to be 850 in the FICO scoring method. There are some who have a "near" perfect credit score of above 820; however, a CEO of one of the credit bureaus disclosed that in all his years at the bureau, he had "never seen" an 850 credit score.

No one is perfect, so do not hold yourself to the impossible task of obtaining a credit score of 850. Anything over an 800 will get you really anything you want credit wise. Having such a high score can take eight years or more as one of the scoring criteria is length of credit history.

A credit history with average accounts of eight years or more is considered the best rating in this area. So if you are young or just now starting to repair your credit, set realistic goals for yourself. But for the best scores, you will need several credit accounts with perfect payment history, excellent debt to credit ratios, low to no inquires, with history of longevity with your creditors. It does take time. The best thing to do here is to decide what your goal is for obtaining credit and set a goal for a credit score that is in line with your desired end result.

Credit Monitoring:

There are many websites out there that advertise credit monitoring. There is a misconception that these are your "true" credit score. What many people understand to believe is their "true" credit score is the FICO (Fair Issac Corporation) score. As of the date of writing this, the FICO is the most widely used score to determine credit rating scoring from 350 to 850.

A FICO score above 750 will most likely allow you to obtain most if not all loan requests assuming other criterion is met. A score above 800 can qualify you for "no documentation" loans which are where you don't have to prove any income. Scores below 580 generally won't allow for loan approval or if you are approved, the interest rates are at the high end of the usury law that is allowed.

In most cases a FICO score of 620 or better is needed for home loans, though there are some company that will approve a loan with a score as low as 580, but I'm not sure that obtaining such loan is in the best interest of the consumer due to the large amount of the loan and the higher interest rate.

A FICO score can only be obtained from a company licensed to sell FICO since it is protected by law. Many website claiming to provide your credit score is not your FICO. It is more likely a Plus Score, Vantage Score, or other score. The Plus Score is the credit score that free websites like www.creditkarma.com ; www.creditsesame.com ; www.credit.com ; or paid sites such as www.privacyguard.com ; www.creditchecktotal.com ; and www.enhanceditp.com ; utilize. The fine print at the bottom of the webpage should tell you what score they are using. Generally speaking if the wording does not specifically say "FICO Score" you are not getting your score that is used by around 95% of loan institutions.

As each credit scoring model measures various attributes differently, there is no formula to convert a Plus Score or Vantage Score with to a FICO score. The scores use a different scale and weighs items such as late payments, debt to credit ratios, and history of accounts differently.

Don't be fooled. If you need to know your score to obtain a loan, the leader will insist on pulling it, but you can increase your chances of obtaining the loan and reduce disappointment if you can look at your score ahead of time. Your free credit score will "check the pulse" of your credit, but it won't give you a good credit health assessment. Once you know your score you can pick and choose where you go to reduce the inquiry's on your report.

CHEXSYSTEMS PROCEDURES

What is Chex Systems? ChexSystems is an association of financial intuitions that network in order to develop a database that maintains the records of "unwanted customers." These banks work together to prevent consumers that are poor in their financial judgment, to open bank accounts. It protects the banks, but it is detrimental in trying to rebuild your credit for at least five years or more.

This is also the same system that prevents you from cashing a check if you have ever bounced a check even accidentally with a retailer. For example, a client of mine stated that she was unable to cash a check at a particular large retail chain. She stated that this was the only place that she was having trouble so we pulled a ChexSystem report. The report was clean. When we discussed this further, she admitted that 10 years prior, she had bounced a check with the company but readily paid it. If she hadn't paid it, she could have been charged with check fraud. Since she was never charged, her story is believable; however, the retailer doesn't care.

Whatever link this particular retailer has with ChexSystems, for my client, she will not be able to write a check to this company again. The same is true with banks, even if the debt has expired off the report. Just because it disappears off your record, doesn't mean it disappears in the mind and record of the organization. But you can protect yourself from others finding out about the past poor financial habits.

You can contact ChexSystems at the following:

ChexSystems Consumer Relations

7505 Hudson Road
Suite 100
Woodbury, MN 55125

Phone: (800) 428-9623; (800) 513-7125

Understand that I am not a lawyer and nothing in this book should be considered legal advice. This is a self-help guide to repairing your own credit. If at any time you feel your situation warrants an attorney, it is advised to seek professional help.

To obtain a ChexSystems report, you can go to the official website at www.consumerdebit.com and fill out your information. A report will be sent to you via mail. You are entitled to a free copy by law. This is the first step in finding out what banks think about you. Keep in mind, the links and information provided was accurate and correct at the time of writing this book. You should always do your due diligence in ensuring addresses and phone numbers to bureaus and collectors have not changed. This happens often and it is the company's responsibility by law to notify you of any address changes.

Step 1: After receiving the report, you will want to review it. If it should have an incorrect social security number, date of birth or other errors you may have been a victim of identity theft. If you find inaccuracies or items you want to challenge, make a copy of the report, indicate the item you want to challenge and sent it Certified Mail with return receipt back to the reporting agency and request an investigation. ChexSystems is also governed by the Fair Credit Reporting Act. They have to investigate and verify any disputed information within 30 days. If they do not, they must DELETE the disputed item. This is the ideal situation for you. However, if they do verify the information, be prepared to take the next step. (Letter provided below for Step 1)

Your Name
Address

ChexSystem Consumer Relations
7805 Hudsan Rd
Suite 100
Woodbury, MN 55125

Date

RE: Consumer ID # *(should be on the report)*

Dear Collections and Consumer Relationship Dept:

I have recently been informed that there is negative information reported by *(named bank)* in my ChexSystems file which shows up under my Social Security number. When I ordered this report I saw an entry from this bank stating I *(state condition; ie. NSF, Unpaid account, etc)* in *(Month/Year)*.

I am not aware of ever having this *(same as above)* from this bank.

I am requesting that you validate this information from *(bank name)* and provide me with the documentation associated with this *(condition)* that shows my signature. If you are unable to provide this, I ask *(demand, insist, what every language you choose)* to have this removed immediately deleted from my file associated with my Social Security number.

I understand that by law you have 30 days to complete this investigation per the Fair Credit Reporting Act. I am keeping careful records of you actions, in the event this matter needs to go to small claims court.

Provide contact information

You can also CC: a lawyer, (make up a name if you wish), State Attorney, Banking Commission, or whatever agency you believe can be notified if a violation occurs.

Sign your letter

Step 2: In this next step, you will again send a certified letter, Return

Receipt to the company if they "verified" the debt or information is

accurate. The clock starts ticking the moment they sign for the letter

and again they have 30 days to investigate.

Your Name
Address

ChexSystem Consumer Relations
7805 Hudson Rd
Suite 100
Woodbury, MN 55125

Date

RE: Consumer ID # *(should be on the report)*

Dear Collections and Consumer Relationship Dept:
This letter is in response to your claim that *(bank)* has verified that I have an unpaid debt with them. Again, you have failed to provide me with a copy of any viable evidence submitted by *(bank)*.

I am now requesting a description of the procedure used to determine the accuracy and completeness of the information provided, within 15 days of the completion of the re-investigation.

Also, please provide me the name, address, and telephone number of each person contacted at *(bank)* regarding this alleged account. I am formally requesting a copy of any documents provided by *(bank)*, showing my signature, and showing that I am legally bound to this obligation.

Some employee looking at a screen, seeing my name in their database is NOT verification or validation of the alleged debt. I am making a final goodwill attempt to have this matter cleared up. The listed item is entirely inaccurate and incomplete, and represents a very serious error in your reporting.

Failure to comply with federal regulations by credit reporting agencies are investigated by the FTC (15 USC41, et seq.). I am keeping careful records of all communication with you regarding this debt in the event I need to file a complaint with the FTC and State Attorney General's office, should your non-compliance continue. There is case precedence (Wenger V. Trans Union Corp., No. 95-6445 C.D. Cal. Nove. 14, 1995), related to this matter for willful non-compliance.

Failure on your part to provide a copy of the alleged contract or instrument bearing my signature will result in small claims actions against your company. I will be seeking damages for:

1. Defamation of Character

2. Negligent Enablement of Identity Fraud

3. Violation of Fair Credit Reporting Act

In this event, you will be required to appear in a court venue local to me, in order to formally defend yourself.
Provide your contact info

Step 3: If your initial letter did not produce a response, you will want to send the next letter after 30days from the date that the first letter was received.

Your Name
Address

ChexSystem Consumer Relations
7805 Hudson Rd
Suite 100
Woodbury, MN 55125

Date

RE: Consumer ID # *(should be on the report)*

Dear Collections and Consumer Relationship Dept:

As I have not heard back from you in over 30 days regarding my notice of dispute dated *(date letter was sent)*, I must presume that no proof in fact exists.

You have 30 days from receipt of this notice to respond. Your failure to respond, in writing, hand signed, in a timely manner, will work as a waiver to ant and all of your claims in this matter, and will entitle me to presume that you are reporting my name and social security number in error, and that is matter is permanently closed.

Your continued silence is unacceptable. You must either provide the proof, or correct the record to remove the invalid entry from my ChexSystems file. You are currently in violation of the Fair Credit Reporting Act.

Failure to respond within 30 days of receipt of this certified letter will result in a small claims action against your company. I will be seeking $5,000 in damages for:
   1. Defamation of Character

2. Negligent Enablement of Identity Fraud

3. Violation of Fair Credit Reporting Act

In this event, you will be required to appear in a court venue local to me, in order to formally defend yourself.

For the purposes of 15 USC1692 et seq., this Notice has the same effect as a dispute to the validity of the alleged debt and a dispute to the validity of your claims. This Notice is an attempt to correct your records, and any information received from you will be collected as evidence, should any further action be necessary. This is a request for the formation only, and is not a statement, election or waiver of status.

Insert Your contact information

The next letter should be sent to the bank if the request was validated or if you have not heard anything from ChexSystems:

Date:

Your name and Address

Re: Acct #

To Whom it May Concern:

This letter is in regards to account (#), which you claim (condition). This is formal notice that your claim is disputed.

I am requesting validation, made pursuant to the Fair Debt Collection Practices Act. Please note that I am requesting "validation"; that is competent evidence bearing my signature, showing that I have (or ever had) some contractual obligation to pay you.

Please be aware that any negative mark found on my credit reports (including ChexSystems credit report) from your company or any company that you represent for a debt that I don't owe is a violation of the Fair Credit Reporting Act; therefore, if you cannot validate the debt, you must request that all credit reporting agencies delete the entry.

Pending the outcome of my investigation of any evidence that you submit, you are instructed to take no action that could be detrimental to any of my credit reports.
Failure to respond within 30 days of receipt of this certified letter will result in small claims legal action against your company. I will be seeking damages at a minimum of $5000 for:

1. Defamation of Character

2. Negligent Enablement of Identity Fraud

3.   Violation of Fair Credit Reporting Act

In this event, you will be required to appear in a court venue local to me, in order to formally defend yourself.

For the purposes of 15 USC1692 et seq., this Notice has the same effect as a dispute to the validity of the alleged debt and a dispute to the validity of your claims. This Notice is an attempt to correct your records, and any information received from you will be collected as evidence, should any further action be necessary. This is a request for the formation only, and is not a statement, election or waiver of status.

Insert Your contact information
_____

Keep in mind; you are not doing anything illegal here by

disputing items on your reports. The company must provide

documented proof that discredits your dispute within 30 days,

otherwise; it MUST be removed by law. This is the reason that you

need certified letters so you can prove dates of delivery in court.

Though this process is meant to have the items removed

permanently, in some case the item will be a "soft" delete meaning it

may only be deleted for a short period of time and then reinserted. If

your purpose is to open a checking account, it is recommended to do

it as soon as you receive a letter stating that the negative entries have

been removed.

Not to beat a dead horse here, but ALL responses to disputes must be made within 30 days from receiving the letter. They must send you proof that the item/debt is legitimate with tangible evidence. Even if they validate the claim, they must report to ChexSystems that you have disputed the item and this need to be updated in ChexSystems. If they fail to do this, then you have a case for violation of the Fair Credit Reporting Act, Section 623. To verify whether or not they reported this dispute, you must make a new request for your ChexSystems report after 30 days from the date of that your letter has been received by the bank.

With this method, you are leveraging the law to work for you. The banks and institutions are REQUIRED by law to follow appropriate procedure and whether or not the debt item is yours, if they fail to report the dispute or violate the law in anyway, then your negative item must be deleted making the fact whether or not the debt is yours irrelevant. Because institutions are overwhelmed with mail and phone calls every day, the process often breaks down and they cannot keep up with the demand. This is your "OUT".

In many cases, if you file a claim in small claims court for violations, the banks will settle, many times over the phone, in order to avoid the cost of sending a high priced lawyer to dispute one claim from one customer for a small amount. You can win because you sent all the certified letters and have proof of their violations. Again, this is in the event they couldn't validate the claim or that they failed to respond in their legal time frames.

There are attorneys that will sue for Fair Debt Collection Practices at no cost to you upfront, but you must find them. When you sue someone and win, the company is required to pay your "reasonable" attorney fees. You really have nothing to lose if you have a valid lawsuit. Remember earlier I said that there are hundreds of lawsuits filed every day against reporting companies? This is why.

If you are not computer savvy or you are not good at developing letters or proof reading, have someone read over the letters before you send them to the companies to ensure you deleted all the necessary comments or inaccurate information. You don't want the company to look poorly on you and not take you seriously.

For further information on your rights here, you can reference Section 623 of the Fair Credit Reporting Act and Section 807 of the Fair Debt Collection Practices Act. Each violation can get you $1000 of the creditors/institutions hard earned money.

If you want to take on ChexSystems in court, you could still end up winning. Most of the time, again they do not want to send their expensive lawyers in for a such a small claim so they may settle or not show up for court at all resulting a default judgment to your benefit. You may or may not get cash settlement, but you can very likely get your negative information deleted, which is all you wanted to begin with during this process.

There is no way that ChexSystem could validate a debt that a bank could not validate. If this was the case, they did not follow proper investigation process and is in violation. TransUnion was sued successfully in 1996/97 for a similar practice. You can find case law on the subject to help support your case.

Many people are not aware that ChexSystem exists or that it has such an impact on your financial life. Not one of my clients thus far was aware that they could even check what was on their ChexSystem files. It is a bit of a secret with Credit Repair Companies which they charge an extra fee for in many cases to help dispute. Again, a dispute like this may not be hard to accomplish, but it does take time. So again, Be Patient.

On the pages below, you will find copies of letters to help assist you in disputing your own credit reports. Take them as a general idea and personalize, re-word, or re-write them. These have firm language but you might get the same result with softer language. "You catch more flies with honey than vinegar." This may work in this case, but if it doesn't then the firmer language is suggested.

This is a letter for a basic Dispute of inaccurate items on your credit report.

Your Name
Address

Previous Address: *if less than 3 years*

Telephone number

DOB:
SS#:

Address of credit Bureau
TransUnion Consumer Relations
PO Box 2000
Chester, PA 19022-2000 *or*

Experian / NCAC
P.O. Box 9701
Allen, TX 75013-9701 *or*

Equifax Information Services LLC
P.O. Box 740256
Atlanta, GA 30374

Date:

Re: Letter to Remove Inaccurate Credit Information:
Report #: If Applicable

To Whom It May Concern:

I received a copy of my credit report and found the following item(s) to be errors. See the attached copy of my credit report; the errors have been highlighted. Here as follows are items in error:

Name of Creditor: Account #
Reason for Dispute: ie. "This is identity theft", "This account belongs to my ex-spouse", "I don't recognized this account."

Action you want taken: "Please update my report", "Please remove from my report"

By the provisions of the Fair Credit Reporting Act, I demand that these items be investigated and removed from my report. It is my understanding that you will recheck these items with the creditor who has posted them. Please remove any information that the creditor cannot verify. I understand that under 15 U.S.C. Sec. 1681i(a), you must complete this reinvestigation within 30 days of receipt of this letter.
Sincerely yours,

_____

Your Name

Delete before sending:
Use this letter after you have disputed with the credit bureaus and they reported the debt is owed by you.

Your Name
Street Address
City, Date, ZiP

Date:

Re: Dispute of Alleged Debt

Account#

Creditor Name
Street Address
Suite if applicable
City, State, ZIP

To Whom It May Concern,

Please be advised I have disputed the above referenced account with the credit bureaus and they responded that you verified this debt.

You are indicating a debt is owed by me to (Original Creditor) for ($ Amount) is in dispute. I am disputing this debt in its entirety and am insisting that this debt is validated. In accordance with 15 U.S.C. § 1692 -809(b) consider this letter a formal request for proof of this debt.

I request you send the following proofs of this debt.

1) Original Contract Signed with MY signature
2) Any and All Statements
3) Any and all copies of checks or payments received
4) Any and all late notices regarding this alleged debt
5) Copy / Accounting of the charges substantiating the alleged balance

Additionally please do not contact me via telephone at my home or any other location. I would like all communication from this point forward done via mail.

Respectfully,

_____

Your Name

HIPPA LETTER:

Since a large percentage of collection debts are medical related, this letter will assist you to validate a medical debt from a collection agency by referencing the HIPAA law. HIPAA stands for HEALTH INSURANCE PORTABILITY AND ACCOUNTABILITY ACT and it protects your privacy by preventing your medical records from being given to third parties without your written consent. The HIPAA law allows you to question your privacy while validating a medical debt and may also suspend reporting the collection item to your credit reports until it is resolved. Make sure that you understand the HIPAA requirements before using this letter. If they have violated HIPAA, this letter may assist you in deleting a medical collections account along with any mention of it on your credit reports!

Your Name
Street Address
City, Date, Zip

Date:
Account#

Creditor Name
Street Address
Suite if applicable
City, State, ZIP

Amount of debt:
Date of Service:
Provider of Service:
Acct #:

To Whom It May Concern,

I received information on my credit report regarding the above named account and as allowable under the Fair Debt Collections Practices Act, I am requesting validation of the alleged debt. I am unaware of what this debt pertains to or what facility this is from.

Or

I received a bill from you on (insert date) and as allowable under the Fair Debt Collections Practices Act, I am requesting validation of the alleged debt. I am aware that there is a debt from (name of doctor, hospital, clinic, etc.) but I am unaware of the amount due and your bill does not include a detailed breakdown of any fees.

Furthermore, I am allowed under the HIPAA law (Health Insurance Portability and Accountability Act of 1996) to protect my privacy and medical records from third parties. I do not recall giving permission to for any facility to release my medical information to a third party. I understand that the HIPAA does allow for limited information about me but any details may only be revealed with the patients authorization, therefore my request is two-fold and as follows:

Validation of Debt and HIPAA authorization
- Please provide a breakdown of fees including any and all collection costs and medical charges
- Please provide a copy of my signature with the provider of service to release my medical information to you
- Immediately cease any credit bureau reporting until debt has been validated by me

Please send this information to my address listed above and accept this letter, sent certified mail, as my formal debt validation request, of which I am allowed under the FDCPA.

Please note that withholding the information you received from any medical provider in an attempt to be HIPAA compliant will be a violation of the FDCPA because you will be deceiving me after my written request. I am requesting full documentation of what you received from the provider of service in connection with this alleged debt.

Furthermore, any reporting of this debt to the credit bureaus prior to allowing me to validate it may be a violation of the Fair Credit Reporting Act, which can allow me to seek damages from a collection agent.

I await your reply with the above requested proof. Upon receiving it, I will correspond back with you by certified mail.

Kind regards,

_____

Your Name

Pay for Delete:

Use this if you have decided this is the best option. You can reword,

retract, or alter this, but DO NOT admit debt.

Name
Address

Date:

Creditor's Name
Creditors Address:

Dear Collection Manager:

It has come to my attention through the credit bureaus ***that you claim*** I owe a debt to your agency. While I have never had the debt verified to me as legitimate by your agency, I may be willing to save us both some time and effort by "settling the debt out" with restrictions.

I understand that you hold all the rights to report the debt to the credit bureaus as you see fit and you can change that listing at any time, as the source owning the debt. I am sure you are aware of my right to dispute this debt and to request full proof of the obligation as per the FDCPA. Paying this unverified debt means little to me if we cannot mutually agree that you will report the debt as mentioned below.

While I realize that your purpose is to collect debts as a collection agent, I am also aware of what a paid collection on my report would represent for me, which is not favorable. That being said, I know that you have the absolute right to report this debt as you see fit or not report it at all. It is only unlawful to report false information but you may remove a listing any time at your discretion.

Please do not attempt to continue contacting me outside of this offer or I will be forced to cease and desist our communication and request full lengthy verification of the debt. My goal is to arrange a term acceptable to both.

My financial resources are limited and I am trying to do what's right but I am realistic about my financial ability. I will pay your company the amount of $(AMOUNT) as "payment in full" for this account. Upon receipt of the above payment, your company has agreed to delete the item on my credit reports.

If you agree with these terms please acknowledge this letter with your signature and return it to me. You agree that the terms herein are confidential and that you have the authority to make such decisions. No payment will be made without written confirmation from you.

Upon receipt of this signed acknowledgment, I will immediately mail you a cashier's check by priority mail. This is not a renewed promise to pay but rather a restricted offer only. If no terms can be met, no new arrangements will be made and the offer will be void.

_____

Name of collection agency

_____

Signature of company officer:

_____

Name   Title   Date:

Cease and Desist Letter:

This is a basic cease and desist letter if you are getting calls from the creditor.

Name:
Address:

Creditor
Address
City, State, ZIP

Attn: (PERSON OR DEPARTMENT THAT CONTACTED YOU)

Date:

Re: Notice to Cease Contact, Case # (ENTER CASE NUMBER IF AVAILABLE, PLUS CREDITOR INFORMATION AND ACCOUNT NUMBER)

To (PERSON WHOSE NAME APPEARS ON THE AGENCY'S NOTICE TO YOU):

(CHOOSE ONE)
Since approximately _____, I have received several phone calls and letters from you concerning an overdue account with the above-named creditor.

(OR)

On (date) I received written notice of the claimed debt, a copy of which is attached.

This is to give you notice to cease all contact with me or anyone else except the creditor about this claimed debt. Accordingly, under 15 U.S.C. Sec. 1692c, this is my formal notice to you to cease all further communications with me. If you must contact me, please do so in writing and not by telephone.

I look forward to your acknowledgement that you have received this notice by [insert a date that is two weeks from the date of this letter].
Sincerely,

_____
Name

NOTICE:

Any and all references to companies or websites in this book are for reference purposes only. Names are trademarked and I am in no way affiliated with any of the companies nor do I receive any compensation, kick backs, or funds from any of the companies mentioned in this book. This is in no way an attempt to receive a profit from any of the companies listed in this book or profit in spite of these companies. Information provided in this book is provided from readily available public information and/or with permission from other sources as well as from personal experience.

The information in this book is worth hundreds if not thousands of dollars of saved money over the long term of loans, interest and payments for just one person. Everything from your car insurance to your utilities deposit can be linked to a decision that was made during a credit review process. Use this book wisely to assist yourself in repairing what is damaged and enhancing what needs to be enhanced. As with any do-it-yourself book, you have been given a good jumping off point for repairing your credit; however, if your credit situation consists of special considerations or is very complicated, it is advised to seek help either from a professional credit restoration company or an attorney. Again, nothing in this book should be considered legal advice.

www.ingramcontent.com/pod-product-compliance
Lightning Source LLC
Chambersburg PA
CBHW071625170526
45166CB00003B/1201